FIGHTING FORCES IN THE AIR

B-1B LANCER

D0812078

LYNN STONE

Rourke
Publishing LLC
Vero Beach, Florida 32964

© 2005 Rourke Publishing LLC

All rights reserved. No part of this book may be reproduced or utilized in any form or by any means, electronic or mechanical including photocopying, recording, or by any information storage and retrieval system without permission in writing from the publisher.

www.rourkepublishing.com

PHOTO CREDITS: All photos courtesy of the U.S. Air Force

Title page: *A B-1B based in Texas takes off for action in the western Pacific Ocean.*

Editor: Frank Sloan

Library of Congress Cataloging-in-Publication Data

Stone, Lynn M.
 B-1B Lancer / Lynn M. Stone.
    p. cm. -- (Fighting forces in the air)
 Includes bibliographical references and index.
 ISBN 1-59515-185-0 (hardcover)
 1. B-1 bomber. I. Title. II. Series: Stone, Lynn M. Fighting forces in the air.
 UG1242.B6S76 2004
 623.74'63--dc22

                              2004011748

Printed in the USA

CG/CG

TABLE OF CONTENTS

THE B-1B LANCER

The sleek B-1B Lancer is the mainstay of the U.S. Air Force's long-range bomber force. It is designed to reach a bombing target rapidly anywhere in the world. It can carry a variety of weapons and deliver them with massive power and accuracy.

The possibility of a new, long-range American bomber was raised in the 1960s. The B-1B didn't actually arrive as a combat-ready aircraft until the 1980s. Since that time, like other American military aircraft, the planes have undergone upgrades to keep them up-to-date.

A B-1B Lancer—the "Bone"—returns to its home base in South Dakota after combat missions over Iraq. ▶

▲

An Air Force weapons team prepares to load a 2,000-pound (907-kg) bomb into a B-1B for action over Iraq in March, 2003.

Several American warplanes carry bombs. The B-1B, however, is one of the "heavy" bombers. It hauls a much heavier load of bombs than smaller, **multi-role** aircraft like the F-16 or F-15E.

The Air Force officially tagged the B-1B the Lancer. But the airplane's crews and friends, in the air and on the ground, know it as "Bone," the result of spelling out B-1 (B + ONE = BONE).

B-1B Characteristics

FUNCTION: LONG-RANGE HEAVY BOMBER

BUILDER: BOEING COMPANY

POWER SOURCE: FOUR GENERAL ELECTRIC F-101-GE-102 TURBOFAN ENGINES WITH AFTERBURNERS

THRUST: 30,000-PLUS POUNDS PER ENGINE

LENGTH: 146 FEET (44.5 METERS)

HEIGHT: 34 FEET (10.4 METERS)

WINGSPAN: 137 FEET (41.8 METERS) EXTENDED; 79 FEET (24.1 METERS) SWEPT BACK

SPEED: 900-PLUS MILES PER HOUR (1,440 KILOMETERS PER HOUR)

CEILING: MORE THAN 30,000 FEET (9,144 METERS)

MAXIMUM TAKEOFF WEIGHT: 477,000 POUNDS (216,634 KILOGRAMS)

RANGE: APPROXIMATELY 7,000 MILES (11,200 KILOMETERS)

CREW: FOUR

DATE DEPLOYED: JUNE, 1985

One of the unusual features of the B-1B is its wing structure. The Lancer is a swing-wing aircraft. That means the wings can be redirected—their position changed—in flight. For takeoffs and landings, the B-1B's wings are set forward. That angle improves the plane's ability to lift off and land quickly. The forward wing setting is also used when the plane is being refueled in flight by an air tanker and in certain combat situations.

During high-speed flight, the wings are swung toward the rear of the aircraft. That angle reduces **drag**, the friction of air against the aircraft. With reduced drag, an aircraft can fly faster because of less air resistance.

FACT FILE ★

THE RECLINED WINGS ALSO IMPROVE THE PLANE'S ABILITY TO **MANEUVER** QUICKLY IN BOTH HIGH- AND LOW-ALTITUDE COMBAT FLIGHTS.

The B-1B was designed to fly about 7,000 miles (11,200 km) without refueling. With mid-air refueling, the Lancer can fly further. On a combat mission in Asia in December, 2003, a B-1B remained on the job, in the air, for nearly 22 hours non-stop. It was refueled in mid-air six times.

▲
With a top speed of more than 900 miles per hour (1,440 km/h), the B-1B can fly in a "package" with the U.S. Air Force's fighters, like the F-15 Eagle.

▲

A KC-135 Stratotanker refuels a B-1B on a training mission.

The Air Force likes the B-1B for several reasons. It is fast, rugged, and capable of carrying heavy bomb loads. An empty B-1B weighs about 190,000 pounds (85,586 kg), but it can be loaded with weapons, fuel, and equipment to 477,000 pounds (214,865 kg)—and still take off! A B-1B can also be part of a "package" of combat aircraft. With its high speed, it can fly right along with jet fighters and other smaller attack planes.

CHAPTER TWO

FLYING THE B-1B

The B-1B is flown by a crew of four: the aircraft commander, or pilot; a copilot; and two weapons systems officers (WSOs). While the pilot and copilot attend to flying the plane, the WSOs concentrate on weapons **avionics**.

While the **airframe** of the Lancer has changed little over the years, the electronic devices that account for its operating systems have. Together these devices are called avionics.

A B-1B takes off on a training flight at Ellsworth Air Force Base, South Dakota.

FACT FILE ★

THE AIR FORCE
REPLACES THE B-1B'S
OLDER AVIONICS WITH
IMPROVED VERSIONS.

The B-1B's radar, for example, can track and target moving vehicles. Or it can be used at a setting to read the terrain below and beyond the plane. The B-1B also has a highly accurate GPS (Global Positioning System) that helps the aircraft crew to **navigate**. It allows the crew to make precision bombing strikes from information gathered in flight, rather than having to rely on ground-based navigation aids.

▲
High-tech avionics help B-1B aircrews release munitions with great accuracy.

▲

The sleek airframe of the B-1B has changed very little over the years, but the plane's flight systems have been continuously upgraded.

For defensive purposes, the B-1B is armed with an electronic package known as AN/ALQ 161A. It detects and counters the threat posed by enemy radar systems that might lock onto a B-1B. It defends the plane by using electronic jamming and a **chaff** dispensing system.

▲

Aircraft exhaust produces heat that enemy missiles can follow. The B-1B has several ways to deflect heat-seeking weapons.

The AN/ALQ-161A electronic system detects and identifies enemy radar. It then jams the enemy system either automatically or with the operator's assistance. Chaff consists of metal strips that the crew releases. Chaff can send false images to enemy radar that might otherwise lock onto the aircraft itself. The AN/ALQ 161A system can also detect enemy missiles racing toward a Lancer from behind.

FACT FILE ★

IN THE NEAR FUTURE, B-1B AVIONICS WILL BE IMPROVED WITH ADVANCEMENTS IN RADAR, COMPUTERS, AND THE ADDITION OF A COMMUNICATIONS SYSTEM CALLED LINK-16.

CHAPTER THREE

The B1-B is powered by four General Electric F-101-GE-102 turbofan engines with afterburners. The Lancer can fly at a top speed of **Mach** 1.2, or about 1.2 times the speed of sound. At sea level, Mach 1.2 would be about 720 miles per hour (1,152 km/h). At higher altitudes, the speed of sound increases because the air is thinner and offers less resistance. Therefore, a B-1B flying at 30,000 feet (9,144 m) might reach about 900 miles per hour (1,440 km/h).

FACT FILE ★
GENERALLY, THE BONE FLIES AT SUBSONIC SPEEDS.

*Each of the Bone's powerful General Electric engines produces more than 30,000 pounds of **thrust**.*

▲ *An Air Force munitions loader prepares munitions for loading onto a B-1B during Operation Enduring Freedom in Afghanistan.*

B1-Bs can carry a wide variety of **munitions**, including general purpose bombs, naval mines, cluster bombs, and the latest high-tech bombs. One such weapon is the JDAM (Joint Direct Attack Munition) bomb. This "smart" bomb uses computer and satellite technology. It can be programmed to hit a specific target before a flight or during a flight.

FACT FILE

UNLIKE LASER-GUIDED BOMBS, WHICH THE B-1B ALSO CARRIES, THE JDAM'S ACCURACY IS NOT AFFECTED BY BAD WEATHER.

During 2004 and 2005, B-1Bs are undergoing a major upgrading of their computer systems. New computer software will permit the Lancers to carry additional new weapons, including air-to-ground missiles and wind-guided bombs. The computer upgrades will give the Lancer's avionics an almost four hundred times increase in processor speed. The computers will also increase the airplane's computer storage capacity.

▲
Although loaded with computer-driven systems, B-1Bs are still directed and flown by people.

B-1B bombers drop 2,000-pound (907-kg) JDAM (Joint Direct Attack Munitions) bombs designed to land within 40 feet (12 m) of a target.

One of the new weapons aboard B-1Bs will be the AGM-158 JASSM missile. The JASSM (joint air-to-surface standoff missile) is a long-range cruise missile that is extremely accurate, even in poor weather. It can be launched about 115 miles (184 km) from its target. That distance allows a flight crew to fire the missile without having to risk anti-aircraft fire in a close strike. A B-1B can carry 24 AGM-158s.

▲

A B-1B drops a Joint Standoff Weapon during a training mission.

Plans are also set for the Lancer to be armed with Joint Standoff Weapons (JSOWs). The JSOW air-to-surface weapons have a range of about 14 to 73 miles (22.5 to 117 km). The shorter range applies to low altitude launches of the weapons. A B-1B can carry 12 AGM-154 JSOWs.

CHAPTER FOUR

COMING OF AGE

The immediate predecessor to the B-1B was the B-1A. Built in the 1970s, the B-1A was supposed to replace America's B-52 long-range Stratofortress bombers. But only four B-1As were ever manufactured. They were dogged by problems, including a lack of agreement among the people who were designing them.

▲
A B-52 Stratofortress releases a JDAM.

25

The B-1 program was canceled in 1977 and never went into full production. Nevertheless, the Air Force continued to test the Mach 2.2 B-1A. In 1981 the B-1 program was restarted. The B-1 underwent major changes, however, and was designated the B-1B.

▲
The B-1B is an improvement over the B-1A and the long-serving B-52.

▲
The Star of Abilene, *the U.S. Air Force's first operational B-1B, was retired from the Air Force in February, 2003.*

By changing the plane's structure somewhat, aircraft designers made the new version capable of carrying 74,000 pounds (33,333 kg) more than the B-1A. They also improved its radar system and greatly reduced its maximum speed.

The first B-1B from the assembly line flew in October, 1984. Two years later, the first B-1Bs were combat-ready. The last B-1B was delivered to the Air Force in May, 1988.

The Lancer's first combat role was in December, 1998, over Iraq during Operation Desert Fox. In the spring of 1999, six B-1Bs were used in Operation Allied Force in Kosovo. Lancers were used in support of Operation Enduring Freedom that began with attacks on Afghanistan in October, 2001. During the first six months of OEF, B-1Bs were responsible for

nearly 40 percent of the bombs dropped by American aircraft. Eleven B-1Bs were deployed during Operation Iraqi Freedom in 2003.

The Air Force has an active force of 60 B-1Bs.

▲

After refueling by a KC-135 Stratotanker, a B-1B continues its mission over Iraq.

CHAPTER FIVE

FLYING INTO THE FUTURE

The B-1B is a fast, enduring aircraft. Upgrading B-1Bs costs millions of dollars, so the plane will not be leaving service any time soon. Many Air Force experts expect the Bone to be flying into the 2030s.

▲

The Air Force expects the B-1B to be the backbone of the U.S. long-range bomber force well into the 21st century.

29

Glossary

airframe (AIR FRAYM) — the wings and shell, or body, of an airplane without its engines or weapons

avionics (AY vee ON iks) — the electronic systems and devices used in aviation

chaff (CHAFF) — small metal strips released into the air to confuse radar systems

drag (DRAG) — the friction that results from air passing along a moving surface

Mach (MAWK) — a high speed expressed by a Mach number; Mach 1 is the speed of sound

maneuver (muh NYUV ur) — to move an object for a specific purpose

multi-role (MUL tee ROLL) — capable of being used in more than one way

munitions (MYU nish unz) — ammunition

navigate (NAV uh gayt) — to find or track a direction using a system of one kind or another

thrust (THRUST) — the forward force of an object; the force produced by an aircraft engine

INDEX

FURTHER READING

Berliner, Don. *Stealth Fighters and Bombers*. Enslow, 2001

Green, Gladys and Michael. *Long-Range Bombers: The B-1B Lancers.* Capstone, 2003

Sterling, Amy. *B-1 Lancer.* Rosen, 2003

WEBSITES TO VISIT

http://www.af.mil/factsheets
http://www.fas.org/nuke/guide/usa/bomber/b-1b.htm

ABOUT THE AUTHOR

Lynn M. Stone is the author of more than 400 children's books. He is a talented natural history photographer as well. Lynn, a former teacher, travels worldwide to photograph wildlife in its natural habitat.